12 DOORS

12 Doors

THEEMEMORY ASTROLOGER

Copyright Page

Table of Contents:

Acknowledgement Page

I love you Mommy.

Mer ee too ShtaMwt Ur Djehuty Ari Tchet Dua Herit Akut Shta Tyet SharrUr TepRa-MutAb Het Heru Naasha Ma Mu Nbr Ka Sita Harmeet Kaur.

I love you Fave.

I love you and give thanks to you, Malachi, for **never** closing your ears.

"God(ess) experience things through us"
~ Sat Ka Nfrt Kaw-t Djhty Netch Netch-t Ra Bakenre IX

Overview

Overview of Book:

This book is truly an honor to the 12th house. Inside, the walls of this book you will find that the 12th house is deeply defined as a place where those who have come before can be honored, remembered, and uplifted. Many people have unearthed pathways and made pathways in arenas that are used *now* as lights for others to establish their own paths. Learning the information that is stored in the 12th house, from more perspectives than the ones that have been highlighted, allows this house to be now seen as an area for appeasement to occur.

Appeasement means to bring to peace. An appeasement is an act of high honor. Appeasement allows awareness of one's actions and engagements to take place. This is necessary when making decisions and moving consciously in everyday life. Appeasements allow room for acceptance and forgiveness. With appeasement, growth happens - mentally, physically, emotionally, psychologically, and spiritually. This is useful to be able to take in the information that one is learning from everyday life and turn it into practical wisdom. Finally, Appeasement is beneficial and allows each person to learn how to be courageous, brave, and trust in oneself. This is useful to know to be able to call upon and use the knowledge gained through the art of appeasement to overcome adversity and learn perseverance. This information can be useful in helping the reader strengthen leadership skills, interpersonal skills, intrapersonal skills, management skills, and development-of-people skills.

Many times the 12th house is identified including themes of seclusion/solitude, unseen worlds and unseen engagements, the subconscious mind, healing, and restrictions. These themes are used and explored in the poems yet to come.

A theme that is strong and useful about the 12th house, is that it is a house that can assist with learning interpersonal skills, intrapersonal skills, sacrifice, and dedication - but dedication and sacrifice to whom and to what extent?

Deeper inside this poetry book, it highlights that the 12th house is also the moment before the Sun-rises; how everyone prepares for the moments leading up to the Sun rising and the moment for the Sun to emerge anew.

Opening Poem

There is no fear here,
unless you create it.
Everything is what you know.
The path to trusting yourself,
circles back into you and leads you into me.
The me,
is a perspective of you.
And the *you* is a perspective of yourself as well.
It is a path of uncovering,
If only you accept.
Your mind will control what you see, so maybe it's time for you all to meet.

Poem Table of Contents:

Poems:

Blank Page

Tree's Are For Shade

Tree's are for Shade:

The Sun dances across the sky every day and the Moon dances across the sky every night.
Though this is a dance we can all see,
It is a very intimate dance that the light shares.

A journey that should be observed by looking at and by experiencing.
Experiencing the Sun's dance involves noting the temperature movements as it glides across your skin.
It involves feeling the rays that grazes upon the layers of the body and the earth.

A blazing Sun with some clouds,
The Sun still can paint us shades of gold and bronze.
The Sun is so divine,
Even clouds can't stop its shine.

Sometimes, the Sun is so bright,
Taking a step away is both a savior and a masterpiece.
Come journey deeper into the inbetween.

The iNbetween

The iNbetween:

Under a tree is where to be.
The ability to be shaded
Yet still be in the midst to watch the procession of the Sun,
As it dances across the Sky.

The shade of the tree provides a different arena that softens the eyes.
Under the tree,
A spot is highlighted
And it's the Shadow.
An avenue that is not quite dark nor quite bright,
But a mixture color birth from both
Light and Darkness.
This shade is to be recognized as a Shadow,
The Shadow.

Under the tree,
The Shadow was recognized finally as a savior.
A savior from the Sun's dance as it grew in heat,
And swallowed the day whole.
A savior who came alive,
Allowing the body to be rejuvenated.

Unnamed

Unnamed:

The ones who are hidden,
We are all here together.
They fill up the room and disperse without a notion.

Never separated, but that's what they want us to think.
They are really not there,
but they linger around more often.

From their scents,
To the weight of the floor as it creaks when walked upon,
They are here even if they are unseen.

As they linger,
It is real and it's everything you think.
From the smells, from the voices, from the weight of the room
The ones who are hidden are always there.

The ones who are hidden are not hidden,
But unseen.
Unseen from the eyes that do not look in- between.
Between is used as an allegory,
That shares about an existing thing.
For one which is molded and now becomes two.

TheeMemoryAstrologer

The Hidden Hand

The Hidden Hand:

There is a hidden Hand that is controlled by the movement of the masses.
How the masses engage,
The Hand moves.
Mysteriously,
Silently,
Moving to its own beat that is guided by the masses.

The Hand is like a puppet,
Being controlled by the many threads that are unseen.
Until they are made seen.
Thin pieces of thread connect into the Hand.
Forming the muscles,
Flesh and skeletons that are within the Hand.

As the Hand moves,
The group sways alike.
The head is the group and the Hand is the body,
For this is how the group works.
The Hand is the group and the group moves the Hand.
The Hand moves silently,
Sweeping to the tones and vibrations that echo off the walls.
This echo is the shift that vitalizes the features and movements of the Hand.

The Hand fluctuates as it glides and slides acting as a pendulum.
Constantly switching between right and left.
The Hand creeps upon its victim and hauntingly is gone again.
Impacting the physicality of the body
While the Hand leaves no trail.

The group controls the Hand's movements
Swaying it gently from side to side.
The sways are not gentle,

For the weight from swinging back and forth.

Right and Left,
Momentum is gained.
An object that is now seen light,
Warrants a new perspective when it passes into, unto the next.

As the group controls the Hand,
You never know where you stand
Until the Hand comes for you
And knocks you in the sand.

The Sand is time,
A location,
And a memory.
The Sand is a physical place that shows no correlation of time.
This is a poem about the hidden Hand,
How it moves,
And who controls this mysterious puppet.

But this is really a note on art,
And how to tell a secret.
Relating to the groups and how they maintain.
For this information is learned first-Hand.
Experienced only by going through.
This is an ode and a note,
To share a tale regarding the personal thoughts now made into shared perspectives.

The group looks out for one another,
But it's not how you think.
You must give parts of yourself to play along,
To make you seem but not as a threat.
But as a collector of knowledge.
Torn apart,
Isolated,
Ignored is just a few words they'll do.
But that is your power you must summon,

To understand the deeper essence of you.
This poem dug deep to bring you further closer
To the reason you are here again.

It is to take in and to learn the motives of the seen and unseen
Whether they are explained or not.

Watch the group and how they move,
For their Hand can move and grace you.
Pay attention to how they made you felt,
So that you won't do it to others.

Once you notice how the Hand engages,
You will see it's true mind.
You will see between the hidden motives,
The how and the why they are moved.
And this is for you to pay close attention
So that you can see the hidden Hands connections.

Play Begins At A Theater:

Play Begins At A Theater:

As the lights begins to shift,
Darkness settles over the auditorium.

The eyes dilate to accept the darkness.
The eyes,now, focused deeply on the stage while the breathing relaxes to the sounds
of the theater.

Each person's breath is resting to the harmony that is being curated by the story that
is being told.
The sounds slowly blended into melodies.
The melodies play an important part in the dance of emotional pulls.

The narrator grabs the attention of every individual
Now each individual is collected as one.

Dreamer

Dreamer:

The Night settles as the Sun does it's daily dance across the threshold.
Dust settles in as Night becomes stronger.
Dawn begins to fade and is transferred.
The transformation is the dance of siblings.
From Dawn to Dust, the siblings dance.
Across the sky and remind us of the continuous patterns.

As Dawn sets the scene, Dust comes to finish.
The continuous story begins,
The other finishes.
The only true friend that Dawn has is Dust,
And the only true companion Dust has is Dawn.

Neither to be separated.
For if there was one without the other,
There will be no ending or beginning but a continuous nothingness.

Dawn and Dust are siblings,
But they are one in the same.
They each have their own creatures who move in their realm.
Please Do not be afraid of the ones who live within,
For they are just the characters of the stories untold,
But yet, a reminder of the ways Dust and Dawn can dance once more.

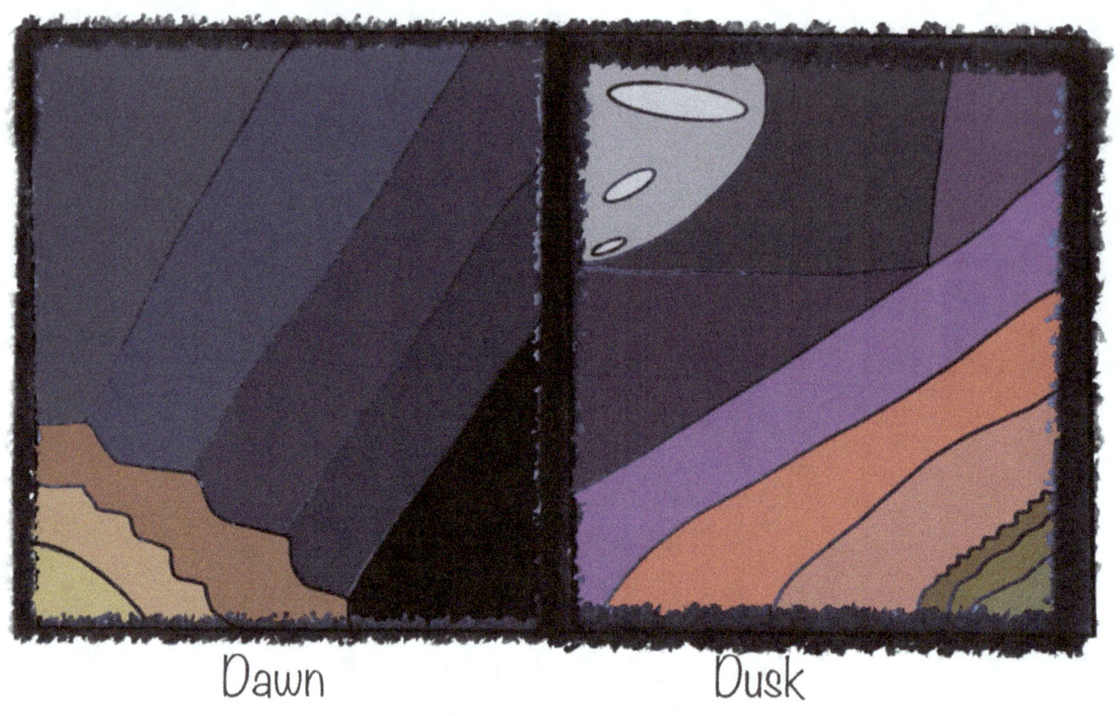

TheeMemoryAstrologer

People Need People
(Feeding People)

People Need People (Feeding People):

Nourishments can be seen as many things.
They may be inspiring thoughts and daydreams.

They may be movements and shapes
That the body makes,
From individual and collected sounds.
Nourishment is defined as many things and may be seen as prayer and communion
with Source.

All these things are decided upon by you,
So define nourishment and what it is about.

People need people to stand in being them,
That is truly what this poem is about.
There is an alchemical process that is often ignored but we all bask in the power.

If we tell you a secret, it's love we really want to give.

When one allows processes to work in harmony,
They must begin deciding who they are going to choose.
When they choose themselves,
This emits a magical essence that is passed to others so they too are embraced with
the spark.

5

5:

I find myself in others,
But it is not like how you look at a reflection.
There is no glass that shines back.
But instead a presence that appears.

Inside this presence is me,
But they call themselves other names.
As though I am not the inspiration,
But they say I am not there.
They take bits away from me,
And say I never had it.

I see myself in others as parts intertwined with their reflection.
Parts taken and reimagined.
Parts taken and remodified.
Parts taken.
Parts that created a perfect whole are now undone.
Shared amongst the masses.

They say I don't matter and what I bring is not what I do.
From the words,
the parts fall and scatter.
That's how I find myself in others.

I see myself in others as ways that people have taken parts of me
and molded it into them.

When I see myself,
I speak but then I realize that portion does not speak back.
I see myself in others,
And they have taken some of me and pulled it into themselves.

When I reach out to connect,
The line fades.
I see myself in others, and they don't acknowledge me.
They say that I am not there.

I see what I have done for others and they don't acknowledge me.

Bits here,
Pieces there,
Gestures are all the same.
I see myself in others and they tell me that I am not there.

When I see myself in others, I ask for help.
Only to come to realize, there will be none.
I see myself in others and they have changed me.
They have taken pieces and bits of me and infused it,
Inside their minds,
Inside their values,
But not in their hearts.
I see myself in others even when others do not see me.

I remember this loop to be able to see myself in others.
When I see myself in others I realize that I am the Inspiration.
When I see myself in others,
I realize the spark that I have within me.
The spark that shines and engulfs the minds.
So I can't help but see myself in others.

I see myself in others,
But when I reach to ask for help,
There is disdain.
How can one take parts of me and not help or reach out?

When I see myself in others,
I speak to them even if they will not speak back.
When I see myself in others,
I know that they have been changed by Me.

From that tip,
I will never ignore ,
when I see myself.

Even when I see myself in others.

Even when I see myself in others.

The Soul's Nutrition

The Soul's Nutrition:
Sleep goes by many names,
Hypnos, Somnus, and Tutu.
There are many levels to Sleep which we must travel through.
As we go deeper,
The Sleep deepens.
Swallowing our minds and leaving the body.
As we walk out the body during Sleep,
There is a realization that it is only the mind,
Only one character,
Only one perspective.
But what is Sleep?
Is Sleep only for physical and mental recuperation?
Is Sleep the way the body communicates confessing its own needs?
Is Sleep a realm to enter to experience dreams?
Is Sleep an avenue of the unknown presenting to each person in its own way?
Sleep like a soothing lullaby comes in and wraps you up,
Sends you off,
And holds you close.
Sleep is the closest avenue where our body is most closest to Death.
Sleep is the closest avenue,
in which one can merge openly to other Realms and Worlds.
Sleep is more than rejuvenation.
Sleep fills you up and prepares you.
Preparing is an action,
Sleep is one too.
An action that must be trained,
To better take in the hidden messages ,
That the dreams are carrying in.

TheeMemoryAstrologer

In The Shadows

In The Shadows:

My Heart longs to be connected to another.
My heart awaits to embrace another with its arms,
With its love,
With its smile.

I imagine deep in my psyche what connection might look like,
How they might feel,
How they might embrace,
How they might smell.

This thinking made a bridge form out my mind,
And I crossed it.
I followed the bridge and it unfolded into a world that I never experienced or adventured to.
The world unlocked worlds

The worlds of what connection might look like filled my head and filled my heart.
A longing thought brought to life in the shadows of the mind.
A longing thought,
Which has now created a world for me and my heart to wander.

I wandered in this new World.
And dived deeply into the unknown and created a masterpiece.

But only to remember that this is the imagination.
A world built out of my own Mind,
That only remained in my Mind.

I remembered once more the creation of this world,
And of how great imagination has allowed me to explore the depths of worlds farreatched,
Or maybe, what I have just encountered are all just memories.

From lives previously lived.
This world will not be forgotten.

The Crossover

The Crossover:

As the sun moves deeper into the the Ground,
And the Moon moves deeper into the Sky.
A sound emerges that only can be heard if you pay close attention.
The sound is of the Wind and the Earth as they collide.
This noise is now a sound that has been transformed into a harmony.
The harmony enhances the listening ears to attune the listener to the melodic notes
of a harp playing.

The melody fades as the colors merged in the Sky.
The colors fell into one another and the Sky was filled with hues of dark blues.
Then the Sky filled with hues of black.
As the Sky turned to Night,
And the Moon began to climb deeper into the Sky,
The rulers of the Night began to dance.

Their dancing makes Shadows move.
Their dancing wakes up all the inhabitants of the Night.
The dancing is only seen by those whose eyes have been adjusted to the plays of the
unseen.
The inhabitants of the nights' moments of movement and gliding are only for a few,
Until they go back to Sleep.
Awakened only due to the Moon's rays blazing into the Earth as it plays a sweet har-
mony.

The Moon continues to climb deeper into the Sky,
And it meets fate again,
Just as it does its final dance with Venus.

The final dance is a crossover and now the Moon has been laid to rest.
Only to come again and shine its light,
When the Sun sets in the west.

The Bridge - (Got To Continue Growing)

The Bridge - (Got To Continue Growing):
Mommy inspired

Double-speaking literacy is a form that was engrained to share a Message.
A Message that is coded.
Coded Messages as poems to enchant the pathways,
So that only the ones who must know will know.
Only the ones who must see will be able to see.

Double-speaking is a gift and a trained method that assist with Surviving.
Double-speaking is a part of Survival.
You see,
Up is down and down is up.
These are all ways to portray a story to the ears listening.

Some Ears listen to understand,
Some Ears listens to deceive.
It is best you begin to understand the Message,
To be able to see within.

TheeMemoryAstrologer

In-The-In-Between

In-The-In-Between:

Between the Walls there is a space that you can go.
Once you go in,
You do not come back out the same.

As you lace your shoes up to adventure into the Wall,
Understand you are not the only one who can enter.

In the wall there are others who can walk through,
And then there are others who can only stay on one Side.
Desiring, yearning, longing to have a taste of the other Side.

The feelings are still felt even when one does not journey between the in-between.
The inbetween is a place,
A refuge,
A savior.
A solace,
An avenue,
And a home is what is in the In-Between.

Here you will find all those who have surpassed the clock,
Those who have yet to initiate the clock's time,
And those who journey between.
The In-Between.

The Walls harbors time,
This gives room for all to merge together and dance once more.

Between the Walls,
There is a space that you can go.

Deep inside the walls,
You can see everyone once more.

The lives who live,
And those who have perished.
This is a place that you can go,
That will take you to them.

You can feel,
You can taste,
You can cherish and adore.
Deep inside the walls is a metaphor.

It is a place that you can seek,
And you can walk in-between
But deep inside the Walls are more avenues.

It is a portal and a time machine entwined into one.
Doors that unlock chains of shared consciousness,
To doors that unlock memories of past lives.

Deep in the walls you can enter and you can exit.
Deep in the walls you can be,
You enter one way and come out anew.
A new version of you is transformed.

13

13:

The New World around was full of sounds,
Creatures,
Movements,
And Things never seen before by these newfound Eyes.

From the Eyes, the Brain was impacted.
Changes that stumbled down in a reactionary affect that modified the wiring,
The awareness,
The ability to control the reins of the moving Chariot,
that is disguised as the Body.

From the Brain,
The body is influenced.
Learning how to move,
One begins to acknowledge control
And focused intent needed to move the Engine.

But one should ask what kind of control,
Is the control needed to move a Body?
An Engine is a Body,
And a Body is an Engine.
Both figuratively and realistically.

To control the Body means maintaining Temperance.
Temperature in all its formats.
From the inside and each section,
Each level,
Each molecule,
And each System is involved.

Once you gain control of those aspects,
It's more that's unrolled.

From the elements defined as
Earth, Wind, Fire, and Air,

It will tell you an Avenue that will be exposed.

Exposed has such a hard connotation,
When it's an unearthing process.

Exposed is allowing one to see,
That control speaks through the body.

Control of each aspect and each realm takes time,
But that is why Awareness and Growth is so useful,
Both aspects allow learning to see Sprouts.

The End.

www.ingramcontent.com/pod-product-compliance
Lightning Source LLC
Chambersburg PA
CBHW080815120726
48001CB00009B/2906